HardOptimism

The scientific proof is solid:
Optimism is a broad spectrum force for good in your life.

HardOptimism points you toward
a tough, forceful, steadfast optimism.
It's not Pollyanish.
Not a rose-colored glasses view of the world.
And not just a rehash of "the power of positive thinking."
This is a research-based set of mental practices from
the new field of behavioral science called *positive psychology*.

HardOptimism coaches you on how to *think* —
how to manage your mind —
which is the most important aspect of your work
in today's Knowledge Economy.
The handbook is aimed at developing *deep strengths*...
like resilience, energy, innovation, and hope...
crucial attributes for high performance and happiness
in our world of unrelenting change.

These mental practices and powerful thought patterns
can make you far more effective in your job.
They build confidence and creativity to help you
take advantage of opportunity or overcome adversity.
They operate as a buffer against
stress, setbacks, and disappointments.
They give you staying power and resilience
when your future is fogged with uncertainty.
Finally, they'll protect your health and overall quality of life.

Regardless of what life leaves on your doorstep today,
HardOptimism positions you to handle it better.

PRITCHETT

The 12 practices of **Hard**Optimism

practice 1

3   Control the life-shaping power of your thoughts and attitudes.

practice 2

9   Assess your current level of optimism.

practice 3

15   Develop the *explanatory style* of an optimist.

practice 4

21   Eliminate the *explanatory style* that pessimists use.

practice 5

27   Recognize and dispute pessimistic thoughts.

practice 6

33   Use *positive reappraisal* to handle problems and disappointments.

practice 7

39   Make hope a habit.

practice 8

45   Know how and when to use negative thinking.

practice 9

51   Practice gratitude and forgiveness.

practice 10

57   Play to your *signature strengths*.

practice 11

63   Go for *flow.*

practice 12

69   Act the way you want to feel.

W. Clement Stone made this knockout observation a good half century ago:

"There's very little difference in people. But that little difference makes a big difference. The little difference is attitude. The big difference is whether it's positive or negative."

Control the life-shaping power
of your
THOUGHTS AND ATTITUDES.

The Scientific Argument for Optimism

There's a hot new field of research in the behavioral sciences. It's called *positive psychology,* and it's proving that attitude profoundly affects performance. Study after study spells out the benefits: Optimists get paid more, are healthier, win more elections, live longer, plus are better at dealing with uncertainty and change.

A lot of people have pretty much felt this at a gut level. What's new is the confirming evidence from sophisticated research. It highlights the power of our thinking patterns, and shows the broad influence optimism has on personal effectiveness, happiness, and overall health.

Now we've got hard data. Science proves that optimism is a huge asset—for you as a person, or as a cultural trait that cuts across the whole organization.

Optimism vs. Pessimism: The Payoff

Why is optimism so valuable?

An attitude of positive expectancy energizes us and calls out our potential. It heightens our awareness of opportunity. Optimism points a powerful beam of light into the darker corners of our lives, revealing possibilities that are hiding in the shadows. The positive-minded person interprets events from the angle of hope, finding benefits and creative solutions the pessimist overlooks.

Compare that to the price tag that pessimism carries.

A negative frame of mind saps your energy, as well as the energy of people around you. It weakens your confidence. It hurts your creativity and problem-solving skills. You end up focusing on obstacles, and that interferes with your ability to spot opportunities. Finally, pessimism drains the joy out of life, leaving you emotionally spent and less effective in dealing with others.

Building Psychological Muscle

The good news? *Optimism can be learned. Practiced. We can develop it, much like any other skill.*

First, let's make a clear distinction between "hard optimism" and the old-time "power of positive thinking." Research shows that the real muscle in hard optimism doesn't come from merely repeating positive statements to ourselves. Instead, it comes when we change how we deal with our negative thoughts and feelings.

Let's put it a different way: Positive thinking is important, but *non-negative thinking* is the essence of hard optimism. The secret is to manage the way we explain situations to ourselves—especially when we experience failure, difficulties, uncertainty, or loss, but also as we encounter opportunity and success.

Psychologists have discovered that optimism and pessimism are not two poles on a single scale. They're two quite separate dimensions. And the best results seem to come when we consciously reshape our mental activity that's pessimistic.

Hard optimism represents a disciplined, deliberate way of thinking about whatever life throws at us. It's about focusing on blessings rather than bad things…emphasizing opportunities instead of obstacles…explaining events to ourselves in a way that enhances performance and improves our quality of life.

You're the Boss of Your Attitude

Nobody can do our thinking for us.

Optimism or pessimism—ultimately, it's your choice. You get to decide how you want to frame events. You choose how you'll interpret circumstances. Each of us is the engineer of our emotional life, the architect of our own happiness.

There's a lot riding on this issue of attitude...design optimistically.

"What an interesting life I had.
And how I wish I had realized
it sooner."

— Collette

Which is more important — what's happening to you, or how you're handling the situation?

Dr. Karl Menninger said,

"Attitudes are more important than facts."

We can't always control what the world brings our way, but we're free to manage our thoughts and moods. This gives us the chance to rise above circumstances.

All of us live with an ever-changing mixture of experiences, things that range from good, to bad, to still uncertain. But regardless of the hand life deals us, optimism is the psychological trump card that helps us win.

Assess your
current level
OF OPTIMISM.

How Much Optimism Did You Inherit?

Psychologists figure that about 50 percent of almost any personality trait you have is inherited. Some researchers say that for optimism it's less, maybe like 25 percent. The point is, a part of your positive nature is programmed by your biological parents. It's written into your DNA. The rest develops over time—shaped by your early upbringing, plus the influence of life's ups and downs.

Some people are born with an emotional thermostat set high for optimism. They come into the world buoyant. Bright-spirited. Sure, they have their mood swings. But these fluctuations mainly occur in the higher end of the emotional range. At the other extreme we find the natural born pessimists. These folks seem genetically hard-wired for worry and worst case thinking. With their thermostat set for high negativism, they have to make a more deliberate effort to be positive-minded.

Most of us fall somewhere in the middle. But regardless of how DNA helped design your emotional makeup, you can acquire the skills of hard optimism.

The Influence of Age and Gender

It's likely that you were most positive in spirit when very young. Children rank particularly high on optimism, but it drops off significantly once they enter puberty.

Females in general are more optimistic than males. But...they're also more pessimistic. Studies show that, on average, they have a greater emotional range than males—higher highs, and lower lows. Depression, for example, is far more prevalent in women than men.

It's also well established that our optimism ebbs and flows over the course of a 24-hour day. It's linked somehow to our bodies' circadian rhythms. You're most likely to feel pessimistic, worried, even depressed if you awake in the wee morning hours, like from 3:30 to 5:30 a.m. Whenever you're sick, or very tired, your attitude is also likely to sag. Your mood is most likely to peak on optimism in the late morning or early evening hours.

Fate Doesn't Determine Our Emotional Fortune

What's fascinating is how our attitude habits override the influence of external events. For example, people with a pessimistic bent soon revert to hand wringing and gloomy thoughts even if they win the lottery. Optimists typically regain their happiness and upbeat manner even if they experience serious illness or other setbacks.

All of us can point to examples of people who should be happy but aren't. Or to others who have good reason for depression and despair, yet who remain cheerful and optimistic about the future. For the most part, external conditions don't call the shots on our emotions. We do.

Control the Controllables

Sure, circumstances can affect your attitude. DNA also has its say in who you are and how you feel. But your own consciousness bats last.

Change the way you look at life, and you literally shape a different life for yourself. By controlling your mind—orienting toward optimism—you can significantly improve your performance and overall happiness.

"Be careful how you interpret
the world: It is like that."
— Eric Heller

Life tests us — sometimes with problems, on other occasions with opportunities. The first question on life's many exams, though, is always the same:

"How will you explain the situation to yourself — with a positive or negative point of view?"

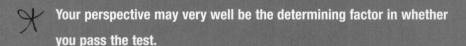 Your perspective may very well be the determining factor in whether you pass the test.

*Lost keep
and*

Develop the
explanatory style
OF AN OPTIMIST.

The Invisible Fortune Teller Inside

Each of us has an inner voice that only we can hear. This invisible, silent self speaks to us in private through our thoughts. It tells us how to size up the situation at hand…how to interpret events. The voice explains to us its version of what's going on, how well we're handling the situation, and how it all probably will turn out for us.

While we're still small children—say by the age of eight—the kinds of interpretations we give ourselves become a habit. Our inner voice develops a particular style of explaining, and it's like a self-fulfilling prophecy.

Those of us who end up with an optimistic explanatory style have an inner self that affirms our ability and predicts good fortune. But if we're burdened with a pessimistic explanatory style, we have an inner voice that criticizes our performance and warns of trouble to come. Both voices tend to be right. Why? Because they help create the very conditions of which they speak. What we say to ourselves counts—our thoughts shape our experiences and literally help create our future.

practice 3

*temporary
self-confidence*

How Optimists Interpret Bad Events

Researchers have identified key aspects of the optimistic mindset.
When trouble hits, for example, optimists have a natural tendency
to explain the problem to themselves as <u>temporary</u>. They experience
disappointments just like everyone else, but expect them to be
short-lived. Bad events are interpreted as likely to be a passing thing,
surely followed by better times. Instead of bogging down in the
dilemma, optimists shake it off and move on down the road.

transient

The second key aspect of optimists' explanatory style protects their self-
confidence. Rather than condemn themselves for foul-ups and failures,
they look for how other factors or circumstances might have contributed
to the problem. The optimists' self-esteem remains strong because they
don't beat themselves up with blame—they seek to <u>externalize</u> it.

*external
not
personal*

Optimists also make a habit of putting boundaries around their <u>fears</u>
and failures. This involves looking at trouble as being limited in nature.
For example, seeing it as a single problem…or unique to a specific
situation…and not likely to have a generalized damaging effect. This
simplifies problems and keeps the optimists from blowing bad things
out of proportion.

specific

Interpreting difficulties this way gives the optimists a sense of control.
They approach adversity and uncertainty with faith in their ability
to handle the situation…to deal…to make a difference. Instead of
concluding that they're helpless, they proceed as if they can influence
the outcome.

By looking at bad events as *transient, external,* and *specific to the
situation at hand,* life just appears more promising. The optimists give
themselves an edge because their world doesn't seem so threatening.

16

The Optimists' Slant on Good Events

The explanations optimists give for good events reveal a quite different reasoning process.

While they rely on *external* reasons to explain away setbacks, they're good at finding *internal* reasons to account for their successes. Defeat, for example, may be blamed on bad luck. But winning isn't dismissed as merely due to good luck. Optimists take personal credit for causing favorable outcomes. They tell themselves, "I succeeded because of my traits or special abilities," whereas a pessimist might say, "I just got a lucky break."

Explaining success this way implies that the causes of good fortune are lasting, not fleeting. In fact, when things go their way, optimists routinely attribute it to causes that are stable and long-lived, maybe *permanent.* They also view the causes as likely to have a *pervasive* influence. In their thinking, the causes of a particular success are likely to contribute to an even broader range of benefits.

Seeing the causes of good events as *long-lasting, internal,* and *pervasive* nurtures a favorable self-image. This explanatory style also helps optimists maintain their positive outlook.

The Power of a Positive Perspective

Sooner or later we all get hit with problems. An optimistic explanatory style helps us take the punch.

Everybody also gets a shot at opportunities. It could be that your big chance sparkles in full view... it may be that shiny possibilities are hidden beneath a gritty surface of failure and disappointment... or bright promise might be obscured by the vague fog of uncertainty.

Regardless of the landscape, optimism improves your odds for taking advantage of the situation.

"What the caterpillar calls
a tragedy, the Master calls
a butterfly."
— Richard Bach

Research psychologists have cracked the code on pessimism.

They've figured out how it works. They know how it manages to stay alive inside your mind. Plus their studies prove how fast and broadly you'll benefit when you silence this dark side of your thoughts.

In the newspaper business there's an old saying that goes, "Bad news chases good news away." This same problem shows up in the pessimist's head, and it follows a clear, predictable pattern.

Make a few simple changes in the way you think, and you'll have a lot more room for the "good news" power of optimism.

Eliminate the
explanatory style
THAT PESSIMISTS USE.

How Our Self-Authoring Capacities Work

Do you think it's more important to be positive, or not to be negative? Sounds like a trick question. But it turns out we accomplish more for ourselves by reducing pessimism than by trying to pump up optimism. Just like in the newspaper business—good news doesn't get much attention if there's a lot of bad news going around.

Next question. Where do you think most of the bad news comes from that's floating around in your head? Here's a clue: You talk more to yourself than to anybody else in the world. You're also the one responsible for allowing toxic self-talk to occupy your mind. And whenever you allow pessimism into your stream of consciousness, the lights go out for optimism.

Notice how your critical inner voice focuses on limitations, mistakes, short-comings, what might go wrong. It also discounts your strengths and discredits the good things you do. Even its warnings will be offered up in ways that aren't actually helpful, but instead weaken you for potential challenges.

By the way, don't confuse these putdowns and scare tactics with worth-while self-critique. And it's certainly not your "conscience" giving you valuable guidance. It's more like a mean witch in your head who knows where your soft spots lie—your slipups, your little everyday scandals, your deepest hopes and fears. The critical inner voice seizes on these points of vulnerability and turns you against yourself. Under this mental onslaught all the upbeat, promising "good news" gets lost in the darkness. The evidence that powerfully justifies optimism never gets a chance to shine.

Why Pessimists Bog Down in Bad Events

While pessimists allow more sheer volume of negative traffic in their heads, they also make three key mistakes in how they "explain" bad events.

First, they habitually accuse themselves of being the root cause of their troubles. Instead of sizing up some bad event as being just a problem, it's viewed as a *personal* problem. They rush to accept blame, discounting other contributing factors and displaying an amazing lack of justice in the way they condemn themselves.

The second flaw shows up in pessimists' expectations that bad events will be *permanent*. They lock in on a "no-relief-in-sight" outlook that refuses to consider evidence to the contrary. Problems are seen as chronic and likely to persist a long time. This weighs down the spirit and wounds ambition.

Error number three? Pessimists routinely oversell themselves on how far-reaching the negative effects of a problem will be. They don't limit their concern to the actual situation at hand. They get carried away on the wings of unjustified worry, convincing themselves that any bad effects will be *pervasive*. The trouble is expected to bleed into other areas of their lives, smearing more damage across tomorrow that they might as well start dreading today.

By interpreting difficulties as *personal, permanent,* and *pervasive,* pessimists keep their misery alive. Very little mental space remains for optimism.

The Pessimists' Warped Explanations for Good Events

There are times, of course, when fortune smiles on the pessimists. But their interpretation of these *good events* mirrors the optimists' explanatory style for *bad events*. Positive-minded folks discount the implications of problems and setbacks…negative thinkers discount the implications when things go just great.

Here again we see three key flaws in the pessimists' thinking patterns:

- They deny themselves credit for bringing about good events. Their self-critical attitude prevents them from buying the idea that they're the direct cause. Instead, success is attributed to *external* factors.

- Good fortune is interpreted as likely to be just a passing thing — sort of a random event. Because they consider it *temporary,* they can't get all that cranked up about what positive things it might imply about their future.

- Since pessimists explain good events as due to causes that are *specific* in nature, they expect a limited positive effect on their lives. Contrast this with the optimists, who presume that the causes of good events have a pervasive effect, broadly influencing their lives for the better.

If we size up life through the pessimists' lens of negative distortion, even our successes create a weak basis for hope. We get little boost to our self-esteem. Failures and difficulties hit us pretty hard, while our victories do less than they should to lift and strengthen us.

Focus on What You Want to Expand

It's said that "dwelling on the negative simply contributes to its power."

Pessimism can only survive on a diet of negative thinking. Stop feeding your mind these kinds of thoughts, and life immediately brightens.

You can still engage in objective self-critique when it's appropriate. You also can take an unvarnished look at the risks, problems, and downside potential—just do it with the eyes of an optimist.

"Whenever he thought about it
he felt terrible. And so, at last,
he came to a fateful decision.
He decided not to think about it."

— **John-Roger and Peter McWilliams,** *Life 101*

Henry David Thoreau said,

"We are always paid for our suspicion by finding what we suspect."

This points out the primary disadvantage of negative thinking: It orients us toward what we don't want, while obscuring the good that's within our reach. The simple fact is that pessimism increases the risk factors in our lives.

In contrast, an optimistic mindset invites us into a brighter future... orients us toward solutions... energizes us for successful action.

So nail negative thinking when it starts. When pessimism refuses to yield, challenge the accuracy of your thoughts. Clearing the path for optimism consistently serves our best interests.

Recognize

and dispute

PESSIMISTIC THOUGHTS.

Four Enemies of Optimism

Probably 70 percent of your negative thoughts slip past without you consciously perceiving them as being negative. This statistic holds true whether you're a devout optimist or a card-carrying pessimist. This poses a problem, because the best way to deal with pessimism is through prevention rather than cure. But it's hard to defend against an enemy you don't recognize.

Ordinarily pessimism sneaks up on us in these negative c-words: *concern, complaining, commiserating,* or *criticizing.* When we're in any of these four modes of thought, we're mentally filtering our experiences to focus on the negative. More specifically, we're planting the seeds of pessimism.

This takes up mental shelf space that we need to save for optimism.

Kill Negative Thinking While It's Young

The key here is quick detection. It's far easier to protect against negativity in its early stages than to overcome it successfully later on.

For example, when worry first sets in, take a moment to reflect on past successes. Then focus on current strengths...on what's working... on exceptions to your *concerns.* Deliberately change your inner voice from "problem talk" to "solution talk." Center your attention on possibilities. Imagine hypothetical solutions. You'll handle your *concerns* more effectively by consciously shifting from negativity to a more promising mental track.

If you're hit with the urge to gripe or *complain,* put it on hold until you've scanned for a "good news" side to your situation. What can you see to approve of? Appreciate? Enjoy? Instead of bogging down in dissatisfaction, do your part to fix the situation. Or look for potential benefits hiding inside the problem.

Resist the impulse to *commiserate* with others. It's not your job. It doesn't make you a better team player. You won't be rewarded for it. Participating in other people's negative attitudes just sucks all the optimism out of the air. You're more helpful if you turn their attention toward resources. Or help correct distortions in their thinking. Or maybe just change the subject. Above all, don't wallow in their dark moods with them.

Finally, be quick to second-guess yourself when you start to *criticize.* Sure, there's such a thing as "constructive" criticism. But most of the time it's destructive. At least give equal air time to affirming, approving, and searching for opportunity in the situation. It'll give you better results and help you maintain an optimistic mindset.

Learn How to Argue with Yourself

There's also a fifth c-word to consider: *catastrophizing*. This is industrial strength pessimism. You'll have no problem recognizing this as negative thinking…the problem comes in failing to check it for accuracy.

Catastrophizing is a feeding frenzy of brooding about the past and imagining worst-case scenarios for the future. Dire thoughts keep circling through your mind and prevent good problem-solving. You ruminate, exaggerate the threat of bad events, and underestimate your ability to deal with the situation. Trouble gets blown out of proportion, while you ignore or discount evidence that supports a far more positive view of things.

How can a person escape from this attitudinal sinkhole?

You have to aggressively challenge the extreme views that consume your mind. Argue with yourself…dispute your thoughts…demand objective proof. Look for exceptions instead of selectively focusing on evidence that confirms the negative. Also force yourself to use the optimist's explanatory style: "The situation is *temporary*. The effect will be *limited*, not pervasive. And it's due to *external* causes."

If you just can't make that work for you, refocus your attention. Break out of this miserable cycle by thinking of something better. Turn your attention in a totally different direction for the time being. Replace the distressing thoughts with other ideas.

Disputing pessimistic thoughts is the core skill for "learned optimism." When that doesn't seem to work, *change your mind*.

practice 5

Get Rid of the Weeds So the Flowers Can Grow

Remember, the first big step toward becoming optimistic is to stop being pessimistic.

Think this sounds risky or impractical? In the powerful book, *Culture Matters: How Values Shape Human Progress*, David Landes of Harvard writes:

"In this world the optimists have it, not because they are always right but because they are positive. Even when wrong, they are positive, and that is the way of achievement, correction, improvement, and success. Educated, eyes-open optimism pays; pessimism can only offer the empty consolation of being right."

Keep your head clear of negative thoughts. Leave maximum space for optimism.

"The door to hell is locked
from the inside."

— **Kurt Vonnegut**

Like the mythical alchemists who had the power to turn lead into gold, positive reappraisal gives you the power to convert negative into positive... adversity into advantage...setbacks into higher levels of success.

As Kurt Vonnegut wrote,

"Even the bad stuff is an opportunity. There are possibilities there. In fact, I see more possibilities in adversity than in, say, lying on satin pillows."

Use positive reappraisal
to handle problems
AND DISAPPOINTMENTS.

Don't Accept Problems at Face Value

When adversity hits, our innate response is to focus sharply on the dangers, difficulties, and downside. Nothing wrong with that per se. The question is, how long should we let it continue?

As soon as the initial shock wears off, we need to give equal time to the upside. Shift your focus away from what's troubling about the situation, and search intensely for what's potentially good. Reinterpret the situation from a positive slant. Look for possible benefits that equal or even outweigh whatever you see that's bad.

Now this reframing doesn't come naturally. Most of us have to train ourselves to make such a transforming shift in perspective. It requires conscious effort—mental discipline—plus an open-mindedness to the idea that good things hide in strange places.

If you look back over your lifetime, though, you'll note that some of the blackest clouds carried the shiniest silver linings. What you thought were your biggest problems maybe turned out to be the best things that ever happened to you. Positive reappraisal gives you a chance to envision the bright side so much sooner—like right now. This helps you through the stress, suffering, and uncertainty. It also positions you to turn the minus into a plus.

How to Make a Paradigm Shift in Perspective

All of us have had the optical experience referred to as a reverse of visual field. This is a flip-flop in the way we look at something, like when the foreground and background shift places. For example, you've probably seen the black and white picture that shows the wrinkled face of an ugly old woman, but if you stare at it differently, your eyesight shifts to see the same image as that of a beautiful young lady. It's all a matter of how you look at it.

Positive reappraisal is this same sort of abrupt reversal in how you construe the situation at hand. It's a conscious, deliberate switching of your attention from worst case to best case thinking. Instead of playing a horror movie in your mind about the future, you conjure up equally vivid scenarios of potential advantages and benefits.

This dramatic swing in your thinking—the paradigm shift from negative to positive—interrupts the barrage of destructive thoughts. The 180-degree change in focus gets you thinking about your assets. About solutions. About the potential for breakthrough to something even better than before.

Eying adversity from a positive angle opens up our field of view. We start looking at the situation with a broader and longer-term perspective. This reframing counters our tendency to overestimate problems and underestimate our ability to handle them successfully. It helps us regain emotional balance and see new possibilities we haven't considered before.

Simply put, positive reappraisal creates space for optimism. It nurtures hope. It adds to your resilience. And it leaves you much less vulnerable to the harsh realities of the moment.

A Stumbling Block or a Stepping Stone?

Research shows that positive reappraisal is a key trait of the "survivor personality." People who practice this technique have a way of emerging from difficulties even stronger, happier, and better off than before.

Fact is, problems almost never leave us like they find us. Ordinarily we end up either richer or poorer. Stronger or weaker. Better or worse off. Just as wind meeting an airplane wing will either lift or lower the plane, adversity confronts us with a choice. We can grow bitter, act helpless, even give up. Or we can lick our wounds, lift ourselves up, and start searching for the opportunity inside the problem.

When you go through hardship or heartache, positive reappraisal increases the odds that you'll get something good for your emotional money. Granted, the reframing exercise may feel artificial. Negative emotions may pull your attention back toward worry, anger, or fear. You might even think it's foolish or dangerous to think in terms of positive overall outcomes.

Just remember—how you construe a situation literally helps create the reality. And the way you frame problems heavily influences how effective you are in dealing with them.

Learning to Exploit Adversity

Our appraisal of a situation, positive or negative, shapes our very future in that direction. As Greg D. Jacobs puts it in his fascinating book, *The Ancestral Mind,* *"Things turn out the best for people who make the best of the way things turn out."*

Use positive reappraisal? Why wouldn't we—*always?*

People seldom get in touch with their deepest strengths and greatest abilities until it's forced upon them by major challenges. Only then do we really have the opportunity to discover ourselves and the world of possibilities.

"No sense being pessimistic.
Wouldn't work anyway."
— **Seen on a bumper sticker**

Whatever it is that you seek to do, imagine attempting it without hope. Then think how differently you'll proceed—and how much better you'll surely do—if you approach the situation in a very hopeful way.

Research proves that *hope helps our chances.* It puts wings on our performance. Hope also heightens happiness, and is even good for our health.

The key is to be hopeful on purpose. *Deliberately.* Hope is a muscle that needs regular exercise.

Make

hope a

HABIT.

The High-Powered Benefits of Hope

Hope is an emotional force that points the imagination toward
positive things. It energizes and mobilizes us, serving as a catalyst
for action. Because it links directly to our confidence level, hope
inspires us to aim higher, put forth more effort, and have more
staying power.

Under the influence of hope we think in terms of possibilities,
answers, and solutions, instead of limits, losses, and fears. This
positive mental slant brings a valuable dimension to our problem-
solving efforts. Hope also gives us resilience—bounce—the ability
to recover from the punches life throws at us.

Psychological research shows that hopefulness helps people cope with
difficult jobs, handle tragic illness, avoid depression, and achieve
more academically. In fact, a study of almost 4,000 college students
found that freshmen's level of hope predicted college grades more
accurately than either their SAT scores or grade point averages in
high school.

What Happens When Hope Fades

We ordinarily don't give much thought to how precious hopefulness really is until it slips away. It's an emotional asset that we just take for granted. But the profound value of hope becomes achingly clear when we start feeling the ravages of hopelessness.

Of course, all of us know what happens when hope notches down. We lose confidence. Our willpower starts to slip. We quit stretching, lower our sights, and start calculating fall-back positions. The energy drains out of us and we drift toward a "What's the use?" attitude. Our creative thinking shifts away from innovative angles we might play, and instead gets wasted on rich imaginings of things bleak, dark, and difficult.

Some of the most fascinating research on the power of hope has been conducted by Dr. Martin E. Seligman, psychologist at the University of Pennsylvania. He coined the term "learned helplessness" to describe what happens when people give up hope that their efforts can make a positive difference. This condition is marked by passivity, "giving in" to unpleasant conditions, and even despair. Taken to its extreme, hopelessness carries a person into the dangerous miseries of depression.

How to Deliberately Develop Hope

Most of us make the mistake of counting on hope to "just happen." We don't consider it a mental discipline that can be practiced. The schools didn't teach us that this is a skill we should develop.

But hope is far too important to be left to chance. We need to work at it—consciously—so hopefulness becomes an active part of our everyday thinking process.

Basically hope is an act of mental focus. The positive spirit it produces comes when you manage your attention toward—

- What you can rather than cannot do
- What you do control rather than what you don't
- How to best engage your strengths and resources
- The positive aspects of your life—e.g., what's working
- Possibilities rather than limits

We need to practice hopefulness like the professional musician practices playing scales, or like the basketball star practices shooting baskets—daily…with a relentless discipline…and with a fierce determination to improve.

Shaping Your Future

The Visionary's Handbook* states, "Events don't write our future…it's the response, not the events, that determine both our future and our satisfaction in the present with the future we expect."

So give hope a fighting chance—turn it loose on your problems, wishes, and needs. Let it play a meaningful role in shaping your response to whatever life brings your way.

*By Watts Wacker & Jim Taylor, with Howard Means

"What lies behind us and what lies before us are tiny matters compared to what lies within us."

— Ralph Waldo Emerson

It's said that we have on average some 50,000 thoughts per day. Whatever the number happens to be, most of us allow a little negative thinking to slip into our daily stream of consciousness.

That's not *always* bad. But even when pessimism serves a purpose, it still has undesirable side effects.

Of course, much of our thinking occurs in neutral territory, free of either positive or negative feelings.

But the best times are those we spend operating under the influence of optimism.

Know how and
when to use
NEGATIVE THINKING.

How Pessimism Can Add Value

Studies show that, in some situations, pessimism helps us see things more accurately. It actually sharpens our sense of troubling realities. Pessimism increases our perception of danger, sensitizes us to potential problems, and causes us to weigh the downside more carefully.

This implies that pessimism can help protect us in high risk situations, like when there's a potential for catastrophic outcomes. So if the problem you're facing calls for a keen sense of reality, or if it's crucial to consider what might go wrong, the payoff from negative thinking may be worth the misery.

Research also shows that pessimists are generally better than optimists at remembering negative feedback, judging how much skill they have, and sizing up the extent to which they either succeeded or failed. But their more accurate view of reality is a hollow victory. It usually fails to produce benefits that would measure up to the advantages of optimism.

Day in, day out, we're better off to minimize negative thinking. Ordinarily pessimism weakens performance, while optimism enhances our ability to achieve.

The Strategy of "Defensive Pessimism"

Dr. Julie Norem, a research psychologist at Wellesley College, states that some hard-core worriers can't make positive thinking strategies work for them. Instead, they cope with anxiety by using an approach she calls "defensive pessimism."

People who rely on this strategy go through three steps to confront their anxiety about upcoming situations:

1. Set low expectations, presuming things might turn out poorly.
2. Review all the bad outcomes that might occur (worst case scenarios).
3. Mentally rehearse or "play through" how to handle the various problems, and get a clear sense of what gives the best shot at success.

"Defensive pessimism" channels the anxiety into troubleshooting efforts. The negative thinking focuses on failure…what could cause it…how to defend against it. This process, though unpleasant, helps these people harness their anxiety and feel more in control. It also enables them to get some actual mileage out of their worry.

While this strategy might work if you're a rather anxious person, it has disadvantages. "Defensive pessimism" can get on other people's nerves. It also can give the impression that you lack confidence or ability.

Optimism vs. Pessimism vs. *Realism*

Some people argue against both optimism and pessimism in favor of so-called *realistic* thinking. They distrust optimism on the grounds that it causes us to sugarcoat problems, discount risks, and exaggerate the upside. Pessimism, on the other hand, is criticized as too downbeat, de-energizing, and generally damaging in its impact. This crowd prefers *realism* as the neutral and objective middle ground.

Frankly, these folks have surface logic on their side. Realistic thinking sounds so safe, so practical-minded and sensible. It implies accuracy…an appraising eye uncolored by emotion…a deep faith in factual data. Realistic thinking just comes across as the most scientific and, hey, isn't that hard to beat?

Well, it turns out that realistic thinking has its limits. In real life, it doesn't necessarily prove to be the most muscular mindset. Overall, optimism is a much more enabling attitude. Optimism inspires, energizes, and brings out our best. It points the mind toward possibilities and helps us think creatively past problems.

Let's also note that, like the realists, optimists too can exercise critical thought. They can be objective in analysis and deal straight-ahead with the unvarnished facts of the situation. Positive thinkers don't have to be pollyannas. Sure, some people are blind optimists, naively positive to a hazardous degree. But we also have hard-headed realists, whose fanatic refusal to respect the potency of hope and positive thinking can cost them even more dearly.

"For everything, there is a season..."

It's true that pessimism, at times, can be turned to our advantage.
But usually pessimism just carries too big of a price tag.

Unflinching realism, with its bland and uninspired objectivity,
will occasionally serve us best. But realism focuses too much
on "what is" at the expense of considering "what could be."
It respects the head while ignoring the heart.

Let's be honest about this—a fundamental but overlooked aspect
of "reality" is, in fact, what we think and feel and hope inside.
That is a power born of ourselves, and it's very real in its influence
on our lives.

Most of the time, and in most aspects of our being, optimism has
by far the most to offer. Play the odds—think optimistically.

"Optimism is a force multiplier."
— Colin Powell

Life always gives us a choice: We can focus on what's wrong or what's right. Whichever one we feed our attention to will grow. The one we tend to ignore will wither, weaken, and sometimes die.

We can choose to occupy our minds with anger...resentment and blame...all the things that are going wrong. Or we can forgive—other people, circumstances, even ourselves. We can empty our minds of these emotional poisons, and fill that mental space with a grateful attention to things that are wonderfully right. And optimism will flourish.

The darkness of negative thinking cannot survive in the spirit-brightening light of forgiveness and gratitude.

Practice

gratitude and

FORGIVENESS.

The Importance of Attention Management

Mihaly Csikszentmihalyi, psychologist and best-selling author, states, *"To control attention means to control experience, and therefore the quality of life."* Stop and consider the power of that idea. By managing our attention we can shape our experiences. Here's the flip side: Failure to manage our attention leaves us emotionally vulnerable to the ups and downs of everyday living.

Our work will always involve some setbacks and disappointments. The relationships we have with others are bound to produce occasional aggravations or resentments. There's just no way to avoid being hit now and then by hurts, worries, and random unpleasant surprises.

The trick comes in knowing how to endure adversity without letting it bring us down. We need practical countermeasures, proven antidotes to negative thinking. Otherwise we spend too much of our days feeling bitter, cynical, and pessimistic.

Two of the most powerful techniques for managing our attention toward optimism are gratitude and forgiveness. They're valuable not only for what they bring that's positive, but also for the negatives that they prevent or displace.

practice 9

Forgiveness: An Invitation to Optimism

The tremendous value we get from forgiving comes from its cleansing action. It washes the mind of thoughts that are unpleasant, painful, and mostly unhelpful. Why is this so important? Because the best way to build optimism is by getting rid of negative thinking. So long as we cloud our consciousness with thoughts of anger, resentment, or revenge, the positive rays cannot shine through to light up our lives.

Of course, sometimes it's okay to get angry. Even appropriate. But how long are you going to carry a grudge? Two hours? A couple of weeks? Are you going to lug it around for years, maybe carry it with you into your grave? What are you getting out of it that's worth the haul? And how can that possibly compare to the benefits you'd get by forgiving? Certainly we need to *learn* from bad experiences. But we can hang onto those lessons even as we let go of the negative emotions that poison us inside.

The harder the hit, and the greater the heartbreak or loss, the more time it usually takes to reach a forgiving state of mind. But if you can let the negative feeling go—somehow shake it off and get past it—the forgiving will lift you emotionally and create a surge of positive energy.

Sometimes people sink into grief instead of getting angry. And grieving can be a natural part of the healing process. But when we get stuck there, grieving merely sustains our misery and prolongs our feelings of loss. Forgiveness may be a far better medicine, enabling you to make peace with the situation and move on with your life.

The available research evidence conveys the therapeutic value of forgiveness. It's an adaptive behavior that serves both our physical health and our psychological well-being.

Find Time for Gratitude

Ordinarily we find it easier to be grateful than forgiving. Gratitude merely requires that we pay attention to the good things that are happening to us and feel a true sense of appreciation for them.

What interferes is our tendency to take things for granted. It's just human nature for our attention to gravitate toward needs and wants that are unfulfilled. Instead of feeling thankful for all that's going well, our minds focus on what's missing or what we wish were better still.

We're also prone to become preoccupied with our problems and let "bad news drive the good news away." The hassles and complaints of day-to-day life come at us with so much noise and urgency that our attention gets pulled away from things that are quietly "working." As a result, our thoughts often don't angle toward gratitude unless we aim attention there deliberately.

Why put forth the effort? Well, there's a lot more to be gained from being grateful than you might think. Managing your outlook toward appreciation and thankfulness feeds the soul. It brings calm and contentment. It lifts your levels of happiness and hope. Gratitude will amplify your positive recollections about times past, and that in turn sets the stage for optimism about the future.

practice 9

Earning the Right to Optimism

At any given point in time—right now, or whenever—we should have no problem finding things that fit into the "what's right" and "what's wrong" categories of our lives. Question is, what can we personally do to amplify the positives and modulate the negatives?

Sure, optimism might flow our way free of any purposeful effort on our part. But why not put forth a decent effort to ensure its arrival and give it a larger role in today's experience of living?

Start with a little forgiveness. Instead of clinging to some anger or resentment, holding it to your heart as if it were precious rather than punishing, choose to forgive. Then center attention on some aspect of your here-and-now that deserves deeply felt gratefulness—most likely something you've been taking for granted. For maximum potency, put your thoughts of appreciation into words and go public with your feelings.

Gratitude and forgiveness change us on the inside. And they secure for us a future that's more highly charged with optimism.

HardOptimism

"It is astonishing how short a time it takes for very wonderful things to happen."

— Frances Hodgson Burnett

Looking for a natural turn-on? Want something that will lift your spirits and maximize your effectiveness?

No problem. Just spend time practicing your greatest strengths.

Invest yourself where you really shine—call on your very best talents—and watch how it boosts your level of optimism.

Play to
your signature
STRENGTHS.

Get Your Mojo Working

Each of us has a unique, highly personalized set of core strengths.
These are based on our strongest natural talents that have been
refined over the years with additional knowledge and skills. They're
our flagship abilities—our prime resources for achieving peak
performance—so they're spoken of as "signature strengths."

When you fire up these big engines you've got your mojo working.
Things really start to click. You're tapping into your deep potential,
doing things you crave to do and that light you up inside.

Playing to signature strengths gives us the greatest room for
growth...our best chance for high performance...the most promising
odds for personal gratification. When our mojo's working we're
energized and our attitude needle swings over into the positive zone.
Pessimism doesn't have a crying chance.

Any time your attitude goes flat or dips into the pessimistic zone,
there's a good chance you've strayed away from your signature
strengths. And it's a common problem. A study done by the Gallup
organization found that, worldwide, only 20 percent of the employees
working in large organizations feel like their strengths are in play
every day. This means that eight out of ten people aren't spending
enough time in their sweet spot.

Identifying Signature Strengths

How can you know when you're engaging a signature strength?

Well, to begin with, you'll note that it comes easy for you. You'll sense that silky, fluid feel of natural ability—innate talent—which is basically a gift of the gods. In fact, it probably comes so easy that you may take it for granted, perhaps even assuming that everybody else is made the same as you. We often overlook just how precious and unique our signature strengths are because we live with them every day.

Another defining feature is the ability to learn fast. If you try an activity and pick it up rapidly, you could be onto a signature strength. Play with it. See if you get hooked.

That brings us to a couple of other clues. Do you have a yearning or desire to perform an activity? Does it consistently bring deep satisfaction? If it's a signature strength, you have a persistent appetite for it. You can picture yourself doing it repeatedly and successfully. Finally, you find it absorbing, enjoyable, and uplifting.

Build Your Life Around Signature Strengths

We flourish most when we apply our signature strengths in all areas of life. So try to shape your work such that every day it draws on your best potential. Also tap into this rich pocket of talent during your personal time.

Even your personal development efforts should be concentrated here in order to muscle up these dominant talents. Instead of drifting outside of this strike zone in an effort to shore up shortcomings, keep polishing your strengths that already shine the very most. The idea is to develop them into mega-strengths.

You'll get a lot more mileage out of identifying and exploiting strengths than you can from trying to overcome weaknesses. In *Now Discover Your Strengths,* authors Marcus Buckingham and Donald Clifton explain, *"We must remember that casting a critical eye on our weaknesses and working hard to manage them, while sometimes necessary, will only help us prevent failure. It will not help us reach excellence…you will reach excellence only by understanding and cultivating your strengths."*

Struggling to improve ourselves in low-talent areas resembles damage control more than development. It's a draining, deadening exercise. It burns up a lot of energy. So unless you're dealing with a weakness that directly interferes with your signature strengths, you probably should just manage around it. In fact, most of your soft spots basically ought to be ignored. Focus your improvement efforts where you're already most proficient. That gives you the best chance to become an ace and also cranks up your level of optimism.

Where Potential and Passion Intersect

Exercising signature strengths is like watering the roots of optimism. You start feeling better about yourself. You find fulfillment in what you're doing. You develop a more positive outlook toward life.

These beneficial side effects are a powerful antidote to adversity. They also help you exploit opportunity and navigate through uncertainty. Playing to your signature strengths can even turn a run-of-the-mill day into an energizing, soul-satisfying experience.

Want to live the good life? Engage your signature strengths as often as possible.

"Anything you're good at contributes to happiness."

— Bertrand Russell

Ever notice what happens when you lose yourself in what you're doing?

Negative thinking disappears. Pessimism gets crowded out because you're mentally consumed with the task at hand.

Just concentrate totally on the work in front of you. Go at it with your best stuff.
Hit the mental state called flow, and you'll come out the other end on a natural high.

Go
for
FLOW.

Life in "The Zone"

You've been there before. In fact, you entered the zone and experienced flow before you were even able to walk. As a child at play you often experienced this total absorption in a toy, game, or struggle to develop a new skill. Most athletes know the feeling, and they cherish these times as their moments of peak performance.

Flow is that magical groove where our best strengths are called forth and focused tightly on the challenges facing us *right now.* Our attention narrows down to this very moment. Both the past and future fade out of our consciousness, along with any regrets about yesterday or anxieties about tomorrow. Fully consumed by what we're doing, we forget about ourselves and feel no emotion.

In the zone we register neither optimism nor pessimism. If we stop to evaluate the experience, though, we sense a deep enjoyment. Ordinarily a backward look sees the episode as highly gratifying—even exhilarating—and our spirits are lifted. This afterglow may be felt as a more optimistic frame of mind.

Flow is always a visitor, never a permanent resident. Ordinarily it arrives unexpectedly, showing up when our signature strengths are perfectly matched to fit the challenges that confront us. Then, as unpredictably as it came, this dazzling visitor disappears. But at least we're left feeling fuller, happier, and more satisfied.

Nothing but Now

Flow is a live act. It occurs only in real time. So you must learn to rivet your attention on the present—not in some broad sense, like on "today" or "what's going on in general," but on what you need to do at the moment. It's total immersion in the now.

Don't let your thoughts drift off toward concerns about the past. Don't worry about the future. Remain super-focused on what is, not on what was or what might be.

Golfers talk of how important it is to "Be with the present shot, not the previous one or the one coming up." That's the first step in going for flow. Then you need to shut out the noise and distractions. This includes all of the internal chatter. Negative self-talk and excessive self-monitoring can interfere with your focus even more than the distractions from your surroundings. So quiet the mind. Concentrate purely on what you're doing and what you want to see happen.

In his book *On the Sweet Spot: Stalking the Effortless Present,* sports psychologist Dr. Richard Keefe suggests that you slowly repeat to yourself these words:

"now…here…this…"

Using this three-word sequence helps you still yourself, focus, and bring everything within your being to bear on the task at hand.

Serious Enjoyment: The Exercise of Signature Strengths

The reason flow has such a positive emotional influence is that typically we're indulging in our favorite pursuits. We're doing what we do best, and it's delicious. Our signature strengths are operating at a high pitch. They're concentrated fully on the current moment. This juices up the experience, producing results that are remarkably gratifying and good.

The important thing is to figure out how to weave your strengths into the very fabric of your work. To begin with, you need a pretty good sense of where you shine the most. Then you need to get creative and take a fresh look at your duties. See if you can tackle the job differently, recrafting it to better engage your signature strengths.

What if you're stuck in a boring, repetitive job that doesn't play to your strengths? Maybe you can volunteer for special projects... sign up for committee work... engage your strengths during breaks... or start your own initiatives that let you exercise your strong points. But odds are even your current duties can be approached in ways that call out your best. The idea is to reframe your role and turn tedium into activity that showcases your best stuff.

It's reported that Americans actually experience flow quite a bit more at work than during their leisure time. Mihaly Csikszentmihalyi, who coined the term "flow" and has probably researched it the very most, explains why:

"Contrary to what we usually believe, moments like these, the best moments in our lives, are not the passive, receptive, relaxing times... The best moments usually occur when a person's body or mind is stretched to its limits in a voluntary effort to accomplish something difficult and worthwhile. Optimal experience is the something that we make happen." *

---

*Flow: The Psychology of Optimal Experience, by Mihaly Csikszentmihalyi

The Natural High

Flow is all about doing...not about thinking or feeling. In the zone you're lost in the action. You're hyper-aware—there's an unusual richness to the moment—but your moves are more or less automatic. In essence, the "game" takes over and the action controls the player.

Normal consciousness often allows destructive thoughts to interfere with performance. But flow leaves no space for negativity. It's a therapeutic interlude free of anything that might feed pessimism. In fact, happiness literally oozes out of these unique periods of concentration.

So go for flow. It's a positive experience that always leaves us in better emotional shape.

"Real generosity toward
the future lies in giving all
to the present."
— Albert Camus

William James, who's called "the father of modern psychology," said,

"If you want a quality, act as if you already had it."

The principle is simple. Powerful. Profoundly effective. And it offers you an open road to optimism.

Begin to behave a certain way, and your overall experience moves toward alignment with your visible actions. We become what we pretend to be.

Act the way

you want

TO FEEL.

The Influence of *Action*

Sooner or later, everybody gets hit with a spell of pessimism. Negative thoughts circle through your mind. You feel down in the dumps. Happens to the best of us, and it usually hurts our performance.

So what's the quickest, most straightforward way to pull out of this slump? When pessimism settles in and pervades your being, what's your best angle of attack? Remember—you don't feel good…bleak thoughts are troubling you…your carriage and facial expression reflect what's going on inside.

Let's approach it this way. Consider which of these three is easiest for you to change: how you *feel,* how you *think,* or how you *behave.* Of course, all three are interconnected. When you change one, it usually influences the other two. So it makes sense to start with the one that's most natural for you to consciously control. Turns out to be how you *behave.* And that also just happens to be the one that produces the most rapid turnaround in the other two.

Act differently, and watch how quickly it alters the way you *feel.* Change your visible behavior, and the new moves soon redirect your *thinking.* By the way, this holds true whether your behavior tilts you in a positive or negative direction. You can "behave" yourself into feeling bad and thinking pessimistically just as easily as you can "behave" yourself toward a happy state.

practice 12

"Faking It" Into Reality

We may not be happy, buoyant, and optimistic. But we can certainly make ourselves act that way. The key is to take charge of our body language. It's a lot easier to consciously control our physical movements than to go straight at our emotions and try to change them. Likewise, changing behavior is more tangible and easier than abrupt turnarounds in our thinking. So for now let's focus on actions rather than thoughts or feelings.

Start with your facial expression. The brain is wired such that your face is the most accurate reflection of your emotional state. Our emotions are centered in the brain's limbic system, and that's what controls facial muscles. So the first step is to adopt a facial expression that reflects how you want to feel. Research shows that just by moving a small part of the body—like smiling—we can produce significant emotional and physiological changes. The next step is to carry yourself the way you would if you felt like you want to feel. Walk the way you would walk. Breathe the way you would breathe. Talk the way a person who feels that way would talk.

In their book *Mentally Tough,* Dr. James Loehr and Peter McLaughlin lay out these guidelines for optimism: *"No matter how negative you feel, act positive. Fake it. Fake it with every part of you at your command. It's only an act, but act it as well as you possibly can. You will become what you have pretended to be."*

Does this mean you're a phony? No. It means you're taking charge of yourself. You're in control. And after a while, maybe you're not acting at all.

What Are You Practicing?

Just as optimism can be *learned,* it can become a valuable habit. Sure, it may feel artificial at first. You may not be very good at it. But if acting optimistic makes you feel like a fake, just keep this in mind: When you put your heart into it, other people will accept it at face value. Remember, even your own brain can't distinguish whether your behavior is "real" or whether you're only acting "as if." So just stick with the drill.

If we want to get really good at optimism, we need to train toward that goal. There's no reason we should expect to get better at it without trying. In fact, unless we consciously choose to be positive, we'll surely find ourselves practicing pessimism from time to time. That's training ourselves in the wrong direction.

Sometimes the negative forces in life actually give pessimism a perverse appeal. There are times when we get a warped satisfaction out of being gloomy and sad. For example, a "poor me" attitude often gets us attention. Also, we occasionally like feeling sorry for ourselves. But this can't compare to the benefits we get from practicing optimism.

Research proves that our world favors the optimists. So work at it. Practice being positive, and other people will reward you for the effort. Even if there's nobody else around, optimism is self-reinforcing—it immediately makes you feel better and improves performance.

Positive Doing Trumps Positive Thinking

In *The Vein of Gold,* Julia Cameron observes that too often *"We attempt to think our way into right actions rather than act our way into right thinking."* Both can work, but acting works faster.

Start "doing" life the way an optimist does it. Act the part, and feel how your emotions immediately start to lift. See how quickly the behavior begins to shape your thoughts in a positive direction.

Keep practicing this important life skill. Carry it with you always. Let optimism reach into all aspects of your existence—brightening your spirit, strengthening your performance, and positioning you to give far more back to the world.

Optimism is the attitude of champions. And it's one of your keys to the good life.

"If you don't bring Paris with you,
you won't find it there."

— John M. Shanahan

Books by Price Pritchett

- *After the Merger: The Authoritative Guide for Integration Success**
  (Co-authored with Don Robinson and Russell Clarkson)

- *Business As UnUsual: The Handbook for Managing and Supervising Organizational Change**
  (Co-authored with Ron Pound)

- *Carpe Mañana: 10 Critical Leadership Practices for Managing Toward the Future*

- *Culture Shift: The Employee Handbook for Changing Corporate Culture**

- *The Employee Guide to Mergers and Acquisitions**

- *The Employee Handbook for Organizational Change** (Co-authored with Ron Pound)

- *The Employee Handbook for Shaping Corporate Culture: The Mission Critical Approach to Culture Integration and Culture Change**

- *The Employee Handbook of New Work Habits for a Radically Changing World**

- *The Employee Handbook of New Work Habits for The Next Millennium: 10 Ground Rules for Job Success*

- *The Ethics of Excellence*

- *Fast Growth: A Career Acceleration Strategy*

- *Firing Up Commitment During Organizational Change**

- *High-Velocity Culture Change: A Handbook for Managers** (Co-authored with Ron Pound)

- *Making Mergers Work: A Guide to Managing Mergers and Acquisitions**

- *Managing Sideways: A Process-Driven Approach for Building the Corporate Energy Level and Becoming an "Alpha Company"**

- *The Mars Pathfinder Approach to "Faster-Better-Cheaper": Hard Proof From the NASA/JPL Pathfinder Team on How Limitations Can Guide You to Breakthroughs* (Co-authored with Brian Muirhead)

- *Mergers: Growth in the Fast Lane** (Co-authored with Robert Gilbreath)

- *MindShift: The Employee Handbook for Understanding the Changing World of Work*

- *Outsourced: 12 New Rules for Running Your Career in an Interconnected World*

- *The Quantum Leap Strategy*

- *Resistance: Moving Beyond the Barriers to Change*

- *Service Excellence!**

- *Smart Moves: A Crash Course on Merger Integration Management** (Co-authored with Ron Pound)

- *A Survival Guide to the Stress of Organizational Change** (Co-authored with Ron Pound)

- *Team ReConstruction: Building a High Performance Work Group During Change**
  (Co-authored with Ron Pound)

- *Teamwork: The Team Member Handbook**

- *you2: A High-Velocity Formula for Multiplying Your Personal Effectiveness in Quantum Leaps*

---

*Training program also available. Please call 800-992-5922 for more information regarding our training or international rights and foreign translations.

Acknowledgements

In keeping with practice #9 of **Hard**Optimism, I want to express my gratitude to the people who have played a particularly important role in the development of this handbook.

First, let me pay tribute to the researchers and theorists, those thought leaders in the field of positive psychology whose work I have drawn upon in crafting this message and the related **Hard**Optimism training program—in particular, Martin E. P. Seligman, Mihaly Csikszentmihalyi, Julie Norem, Barbara Frederickson, Edward C. Chang, C. R. Snyder, and David L. Cooperrider.

Next I need to single out two of my key thinking partners— Kimberley Pritchett Webster and Stephanie Snyder—for their unique and generous contributions as part of the brain trust here at PRITCHETT, LP. Carolyn Garrity and Rick Wright also have their fingerprints on the training program, while Karen Ball helped nurse the handbook manuscript into its final shape with her wise and gentle critique. I am deeply blessed to have people of this caliber to work with on a daily basis.

There are, of course, many others whose compelling thoughts and comments are woven into this handbook. I wish I could meet each of you in person and express my most sincere thanks for how you have enriched my life.

Price Pritchett

About the Author

Price Pritchett is Chairman and CEO of PRITCHETT, LP, a Dallas-based consulting and training firm with offices in eight other countries. He holds a Ph.D. in psychology, and has spent 30 years as an adviser to top management in *Fortune* 500 companies, governmental organizations, and not-for-profits. His assignments have taken him to Europe, Asia, and throughout the Americas.

Since writing his doctoral dissertation on personal motivation and self-directed change, he has authored two hardbacks and 25 handbooks, with over 20 million copies in print worldwide. Pritchett's specialized work in merger integration, corporate culture, process improvement, and change management has been referenced in most major business journals and newspapers. A compelling keynote speaker, he's also been interviewed on CNN, CNBC, and other major television channels.

Dr. Pritchett is regarded as one of the foremost experts on how to maximize performance during uncertainty and change. In **Hard**Optimism he combines his deep background of experience with discoveries from the new field of positive psychology, offering research-proven techniques for lifting the effectiveness of individuals and organizations.

HardOptimism
Coaching Workshop for Leaders

In today's Knowledge Economy, leaders should become less of a
boss and more of a coach. This "strengths-based" program provides
both the *structure* and *content* for powerful coaching, positioning
leaders to bring out the very best in their people. The **Hard**Optimism
Coaching Workshop shows participants how to develop *deep
strengths* — e.g., resilience, energy, innovation, etc. — personal and
cultural attributes that have become essential to high performance.

Key Objectives
- Embed resilience as a core cultural trait
- Help people become more innovative and opportunity-minded
- Create a high capacity for organizational change
- Build the corporate energy level
- Strengthen performance during uncertainty or adversity
- Teach self-management skills that strengthen people and
  protect the organization's future

Topics Addressed
- Why developing *deep strengths* has become as important
  as skill training
- How optimism drives better results
- Research-based techniques for building resilience
- New performance strategies for dealing with uncertainty,
  adversity, and change

For more details on how to launch **Hard**Optimism
in your organization, call 800-992-5922.